OUR TURKS AND CAICOS ISLANDS - THE INTRODUCTION

A Must Have Book Of Information & Creative Activities On The Turks And Caicos Islands

Author/Assistant Illustrator: Desiree Adams Robinson
Editor: Jason Henry
Chief Illustrator: Kendra Malcolm

Dedicated To: The People & Visitors Of The Turks & Caicos Islands

Copyright ©2022 Cyril and Dorsie Publishing.
All rights reserved.
Published by Cyril and Dorsie Publishing.

No part of this book may be reproduced or transmitted in any form or by any means, electronic or mechanical, including photocopying, recording, or by any information storage and retrieval system, without written permission from the publisher.

For information contact Cyril and Dorsie Publishing, Harmony Close, Kewtown, Providenciales, Turks and Caicos Islands.

ISBN: 978-1-9162967-7-0

INTRODUCTION

The Turks and Caicos Islands (TCI) is among the best places in the world to live or visit. There are numerous islands to explore, beaches to enjoy, and sites to behold. Both the Author/Assistant Illustrator and Chief Illustrator were born in the TCI and after studying overseas and seeing what other countries had to offer; their love for the TCI led them back to their 'Beautiful by Nature' country. The Editor, though Jamaican born and raised, has resided in the TCI for more than a decade; he considers it his second home. Together, they present this informative, fun, and activity filled book with the aim of sharing some of the TCI with you. Whether you are living in or visiting the country, you will have a great time learning about the TCI through the pages of Our Turks and Caicos Islands - The Introduction.

So, put on your reading glasses; take out your crayons, pens and pencils; and put on your creative hats while you explore the Turks and Caicos Islands with us.

And, if you have not visited all the main islands of the Turks and Caicos Islands as yet, then it's time to plan your trips as individuals, families, friends or co-workers and explore this beautifully diverse destination. This is our challenge to you; travel and enjoy the rewarding experiences that the TCI has to offer.

D. Robinson
K. Malcolm
J. Henry

TABLE OF CONTENTS

List Of Activities..1

List Of Illustrations..3

Chapter One: Welcome - Overview Of The Turks And Caicos Islands...............................5

Chapter Two: Welcome To Grand Turk...13

Chapter Three: Welcome To Salt Cay..17

Chapter Four: Welcome To South Caicos..21

Chapter Five: Welcome To Middle Caicos..25

Chapter Six: Welcome To North Caicos..29

Chapter Seven: Welcome To Providenciales...34

Chapter Eight: Welcome To Our Tourism Cays - Parrot Cay,

Pine Cay, Ambergris Cay...37

My Vocabulary Bank (New Words & Phrases)...41

Answer Key..44

Our Team..45

LIST OF ACTIVITIES

Chapter One
- Colouring - International Gateways For Travelers To Enter Turks and Caicos Islands
- Identifying - Map of Turks and Caicos Islands
- Identifying - National Symbols of the TCI
- Review Questions - Fill-in-the-blank, YouTube Research, Colour Map Of Turks and Caicos Islands In National Colours, National Symbols Artwork Compilation, Turks and Caicos National Museum Website Research, Public Speaking (Video)

Chapter Two
- Colouring - Map of Grand Turk
- Reading & Colouring - Lighthouse, St. Thomas Anglican Church, National Museum, JAGS McCartney Memorial
- Creative Writing - "My Visit to Grand Turk"

Chapter Three
- Colouring - Map of Salt Cay
- Reading & Colouring - White House, Salt Shed, Salinas & Windmills, St. John Anglican Church
- Research & Digital Art Piece - Salt Cay Photo Compilation
- Letter Writing - Tell a Friend about Salt Cay

Chapter Four
- Colouring - Map of South Caicos
- South Caicos Video Review
- Poetry Writing - "My Poem on "The Big South", South Caicos.

Chapter Five
- Colouring - Map of Middle Caicos
- Crab Catching Video Review

- Story Writing - "Crab Catching"

Chapter Six
- Colouring - Map of North Caicos
- Exploratory Research - Wade's Green, Cottage Pond, Flamingo Pond
- Question & Answer

Chapter Seven
- Colouring - Map of Providenciales
- Exploratory Research - Family & Kids 7 Day Itinerary Providenciales
- Jingle Writing
- Jingle Recording

Chapter Eight
- Fill-In-The- Blank

LIST OF ILLUSTRATIONS

1.1   Coloured Sketch of Caribbean Showing Location of Turks and Caicos Islands
1.2   Coloured Sketch of Turks and Caicos Islands Using the National Colours
1.3   Sketch of Providenciales International Airport
1.4   Sketch of JAGS International Airport
1.5   Sketch of South Caicos International Airport
1.6   Sketch of Grand Turk Cruise Center

2.1   Sketch of Grand Turk
2.2   Sketch of Lighthouse
2.3   Sketch of St. Thomas Anglican Church
2.4   Sketch of National Museum
2.5   Sketch of JAGS McCartney Memorial

3.1   Sketch of Salt Cay
3.2   Sketch of White House
3.3   Sketch of Old Salt Shed
3.4   Sketch of Salinas & Windmills
3.5   Sketch of St. John Anglican Church

4.1   Sketch of South Caicos
4.2   Sketch of St. George's Anglican Church
4.3   Sketch of The Boiling Hole
4.4   Sketch of Old Salt Warehouse

5.1   Sketch of Middle Caicos
5.2   Sketch of Haulover Estate Plantation
5.3   Sketch of The Conch Bar Caves
5.4   Sketch of Crossing Place Trail

6.1   Sketch of North Caicos
6.2   Sketch of Wade's Green Plantation

6.3 Sketch of Cottage Pond
6.4 Sketch of Flamingo Pond

7.1 Sketch of Providenciales
7.2 Sketch of Cheshire Hall Plantation
7.3 Sketch of National Museum and Heritage Site

8.1 Coloured Sketch of Parrot Cay
8.2 Coloured Sketch of Pine Cay
8.3 Coloured Sketch of Ambergris Cay

CHAPTER ONE
WELCOME - OVERVIEW OF THE TURKS AND CAICOS ISLANDS

VOCABULARY BANK REMINDER - As you read through this overview of the Turks and Caicos Islands, remember to add any new words and phrases to the vocabulary bank at the back of this book.

<u>Location</u> - The Turks and Caicos Islands is located:

- North of Hispaniola (Haiti & Dominican Republic)
- Southeast of the Bahamas
- Southeast of Florida
- Northwest of Puerto Rico
- Northeast of Jamaica

Image 1.1 - Coloured Sketch of Caribbean Showing Location of Turks and Caicos Islands

Region, Currency, Population, Size - The country:

- is part of the Caribbean Region although it is not surrounded by the Caribbean Sea. Instead, it is surrounded by the Atlantic Ocean.
- is a British Overseas Territory
- uses the US Dollar as its only currency
- standard language is British English
- is a melting pot of persons from over 10 nationalities
- has a population of over 45,000 documented residents
- is 193 Square Miles

Islands/Cays, Locals - There are over 40 islands and cays making up the Turks and Caicos Islands.

- Of these, 6 major islands/cays are inhabited: namely, Grand Turk, Salt Cay, South Caicos, North Caicos, Middle Caicos, Providenciales.
- Additionally, 3 tourism cays are privately operated with residences for owners, visitors, and some residents who work on these cays. The cays are Ambergris Cay, Parrot Cay, and Pine Cay.
- The indigenous people of the country are called Turks and Caicos Islanders.

National Colours - There are a total of eight (8) national colours chosen for the Turks and Caicos Islands.

Each of the six (6) inhabited Islands/Cays have been assigned a colour:

- Grand Turk - RED
- Salt Cay - WHITE
- South Caicos - ORANGE
- Middle Caicos - TAN
- North Caicos & Parrot Cay - GREEN
- Providenciales & Pine Cay - TURQUOISE

Additionally, the colours of pink and yellow are chosen:

- The Conch Shell & Flamingos (found in abundance in the country) - PINK
- Sunshine - YELLOW

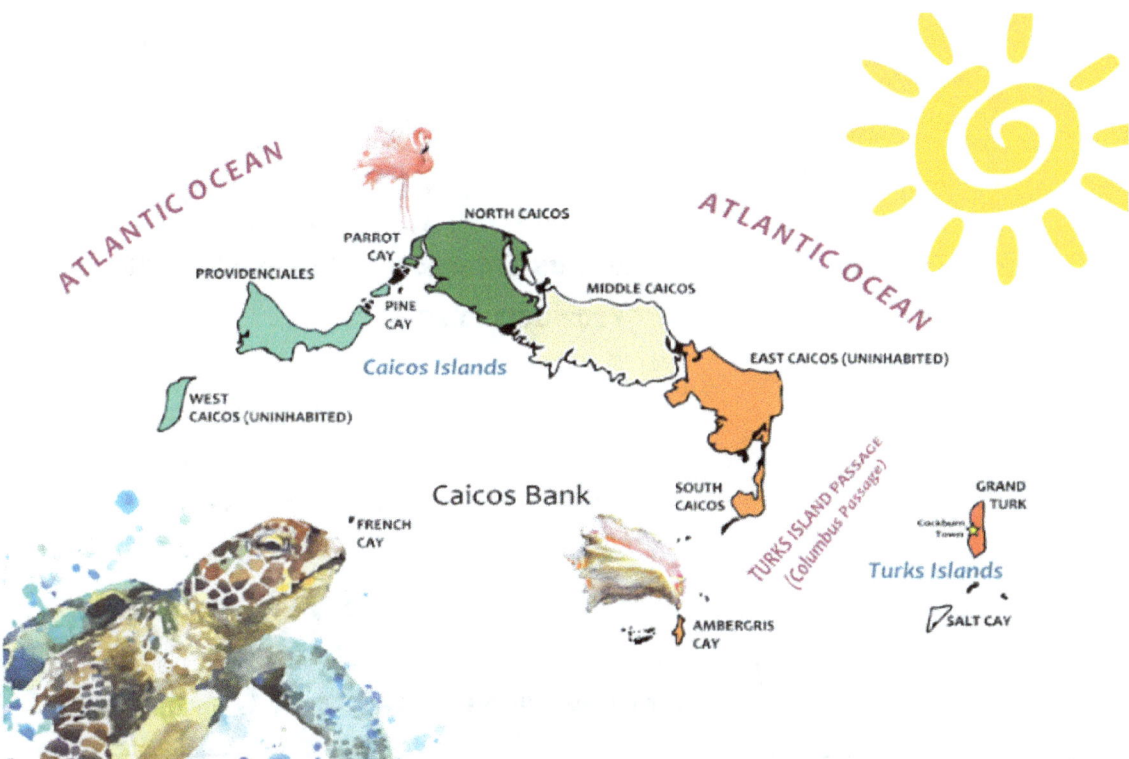

Image 1.2 - Coloured Sketch of Turks and Caicos Islands Using the National Colours of the Turks and Caicos Islands

International Gateways For Travelers To Enter - There are several International Ports of Entry into the Turks and Caicos Islands. The name and an illustration of each is below. Bring each one to life as you colour.

Image 1.3 - Sketch of Providenciales International Airport on the island of Providenciales

Image 1.4 - Sketch Of JAGS McCartney International Airport on the island of Grand Turk

Image 1. 5 - Sketch of South Caicos International Airport on the island of South Caicos

Image 1. 6 - Sketch Of Grand Turk Cruise Center on the island of Grand Turk

Getting Around TCI - Island Hopping - Once travelers arrive at any of the international ports within the Turks and Caicos Islands, they will have options for exploring the other islands in the Turks and Caicos Archipelago.

- Salt Cay Ferry - Transports travelers via water between Grand Turk and Salt Cay
- Caribbean Cruisin - Transports travelers via water between Providenciales and North Caicos; and Providenciales and South Caicos
- Caicos Express - Transports travelers via air to Grand Turk, Providenciales, South Caicos, Salt Cay
- InterCaribbean - Transports travelers via air to Grand Turk, Providenciales, South Caicos, Salt Cay

Note - Middle Caicos is accessible via a causeway that connects it to North Caicos
Note - The Tourism Cays have specially arranged private transportation to each Cay

<u>National Symbols</u> - Several national symbols are promoted in the Turks and Caicos Islands. They are either of cultural, historical, or political significance to the country.
- National Hero - The Right Most Excellent James Alexander George Smith (JAGS) McCartney
- National Flower - Island Heather
- National Plant - Turks Head Cactus
- National Tree - Caicos Pine
- National Music - Rip Saw
- National Dish - Peas & Hominy
- National Pastime - Dominoes
- National Sport - Cricket
- National Coat of Arms
- National Anthem - "God Save The Queen"
- National Song - "This Land of Ours"
- National Costume (Male)
- National Costume (Female)

CHAPTER ONE - REVIEW QUESTIONS - Test your knowledge of Chapter One.

A. Fill in the Blanks Below:
1. The Turks and Caicos Islands is located _____ of Florida.
2. The local currency used in the Turks and Caicos Islands is _____.
3. The Turks and Caicos Islands is surrounded by the _____.
4. The National Dish of the Turks and Caicos Islands is _____.
5. _____ is one of the international ports of entry into the Turks and Caicos Islands.
6. _____ is one of the Tourism Cays in the Turks and Caicos Islands.

*** Confirm that your answers are correct in the Answer Key section at the back.

B. National Symbols
1. Visit YouTube and find an audio clip of Rip Saw. What do you like about the sound of this music?
2. Select four (4) National Symbols of the TCI and produce your artwork piece on them. You can:
    a. do original drawings and label and colour them or
    b. you can cut, paste, and correctly label them

C. Use the Map of Turks and Caicos Islands below:
1. label each of the six (6) major inhabited islands/cays and the three (3) tourism cays
2. colour each of the six (6) major inhabited islands/cays and the three (3) tourism cays in the respective national colour
3. colour the Atlantic Ocean that surrounds the country

Turks and Caicos Islands

D. Visit https://www.tcmuseum.org/projects/turks-islands-gates/ to learn the reason why each of the national colours was chosen.

E. Compile a 2-minute video recording of you introducing the Turks and Caicos Islands; share it with family and friends. **TIP:** Draft an outline of what you will say; practice what you will say; record what you will say and do it with confidence.

Have you updated your Vocabulary Bank?

CHAPTER TWO
WELCOME TO GRAND TURK

VOCABULARY BANK REMINDER - As you read through this information on Grand Turk, remember to add any new words and phrases to the vocabulary bank at the back of this book.

Island Overview - The island of Grand Turk is:
- the capital of the Turks and Caicos Islands
- located to the east of the archipelago
- east of the Turks Island Passage
- evidence of the historical Salt Industry of the Turks and Caicos Islands
- 10.5 Square Miles

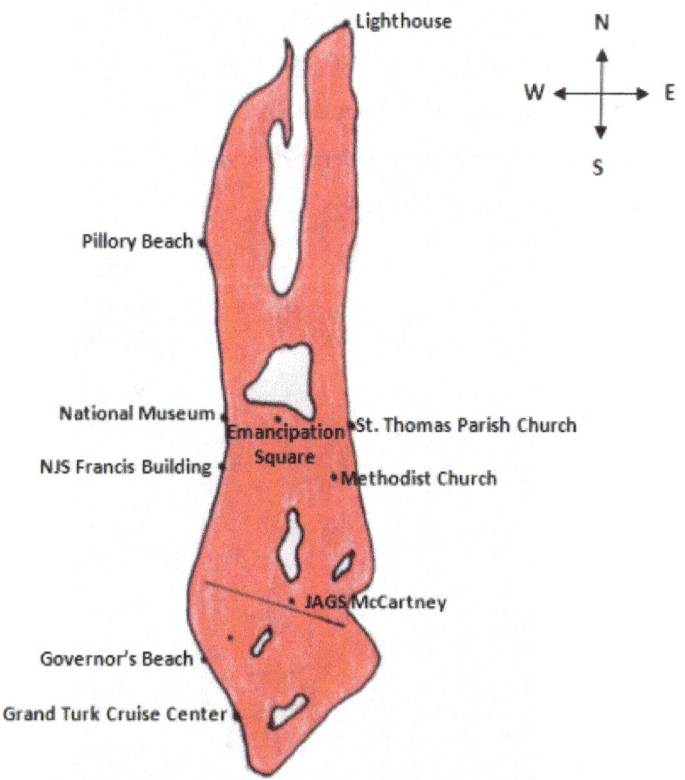

Image 2.1 - Labeled Sketch Of Grand Turk - Grand Turk Cruise Center, JAGS International Airport, St. Thomas Parish Church, Salinas, NJS Francis Building, Grand Turk Methodist Church, Emancipation Square, National Museum, Lighthouse.

National Colour - The National Colour chosen for the island of Grand Turk is RED. This colour was chosen to represent the red fruit found on the Turks Head Cactus that were once abundant on Grand Turk.

Island Festivals - The popular island festivals on the island of Grand Turk (past and present) are:
- Cactus Fest
- TCI Summer Jam
- Game Fishing Tournament
- Beer Fest

Historical Sites - The island of Grand Turk is home to the historical sites below. There are also many others to explore. Bring each one to life as you colour.

- Lighthouse - played a critical role in casting light on the Atlantic Ocean, on the northern end of Grand Turk, in an effort to help sailboats, sloops, and ships to navigate safely. It was shipped from the United Kingdom in parts and assembled on the island in 1852.

Image 2.2 - Sketch of Lighthouse

- St. Thomas Anglican Church - the State Church for the Turks and Caicos Islands is thought to have been built in 1823 by Bermudian Settlers on the island. It is the oldest church in Grand Turk.

Image 2.3 - Sketch of St. Thomas Anglican Church

- National Museum - housed in an historic building "Guinep House" on Front Street. It has a Gift Shop and offers a range of activities such as special tours, classes, fundraising and community events.

Image 2.4 - Sketch of National Museum

- JAGS Memorial Park - a site dedicated to honour the memory of the first Chief Minister of the Turks and Caicos Islands, the late Hon. James Alexander George Smith (JAGS) McCarntney. He was elected in 1976 and died in 1980. (Illustration to colour)

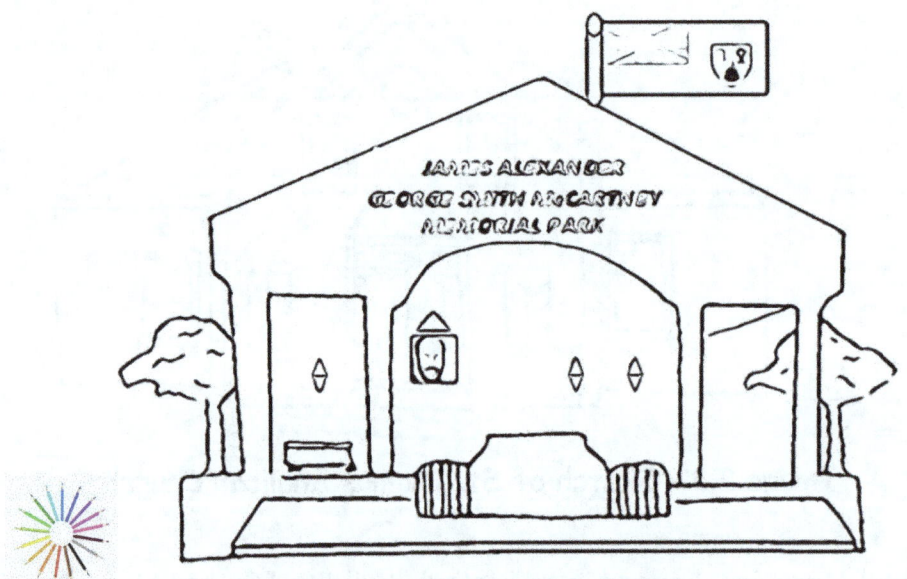

Image 2.5 - Sketch of JAGS Memorial

ACTIVITY - CHAPTER TWO REVIEW - CREATIVE WRITING

A. Write a 3-paragraph story titled "My Visit To Grand Turk". In order to gather more information for your story you may visit:

- Turks and Caicos Islands Tourist Board website at https://turksandcaicostourism.com/grand-turk/.
- Visit Turks and Caicos Islands at https://www.visittci.com/grand-turk

Have you updated your Vocabulary Bank?

CHAPTER THREE
WELCOME TO SALT CAY

VOCABULARY BANK REMINDER - As you read through this overview of Salt Cay, remember to add any new words and phrases to the vocabulary bank at the back of this book.

Island Overview - The island of Salt Cay is:
- the smallest inhabited island in the Turks and Caicos Islands
- located to the east of the archipelago
- east of the Turks Island Passage
- evidence of the historical Salt Industry of the Turks and Caicos Islands
- 2.5 Square Miles

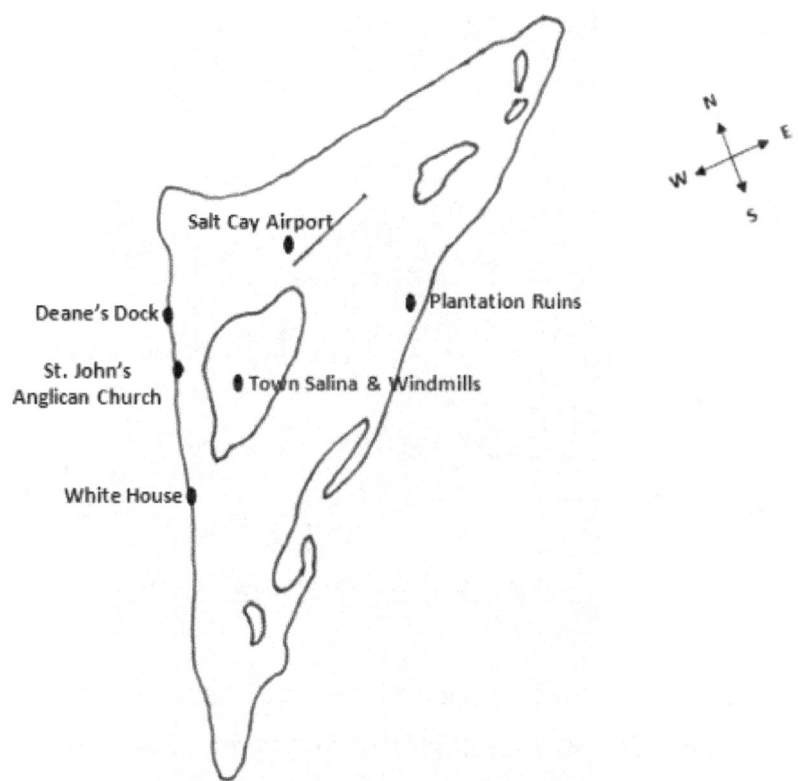

Image 3.1 - Labeled Sketch Of Salt Cay - Salt Cay Airport, Deane's Dock, White House, Salinas with Windmill, St. John's Anglican Church, Plantation Ruins

National Colour - The National Colour chosen for the island of Salt Cay is WHITE. This colour was chosen to represent the salt that was harvested from the Salinas on the Island. Salt Cay was the largest producer of salt for the Salt Industry of the Turks and Caicos Islands.

Island Festival - Salt Cay Day remains the island's only Festival. Historically, Garden Parties held by private residences were popular, as well as Island Dances at the Government's House.

Historical Sites - The island of Salt Cay is home to the historical sites below. There are also many others to explore. Bring each one to life as you colour.

- White House - a historic two-storey landmark since the 1800's that was used to store salt gathered from the Salinas. The living quarters of salt businessmen were on the upper floor and the storage facility on the ground floor. It was built by Bermudian settlers.

Image 3.2 - Sketch of White House

- Old Salt Shed - a single level facility that was used to store salt gathered from the Salinas. Salt was abundant on the island; much was harvested and stored in the Salt Shed before being exported. It was built by Bermudian settlers.

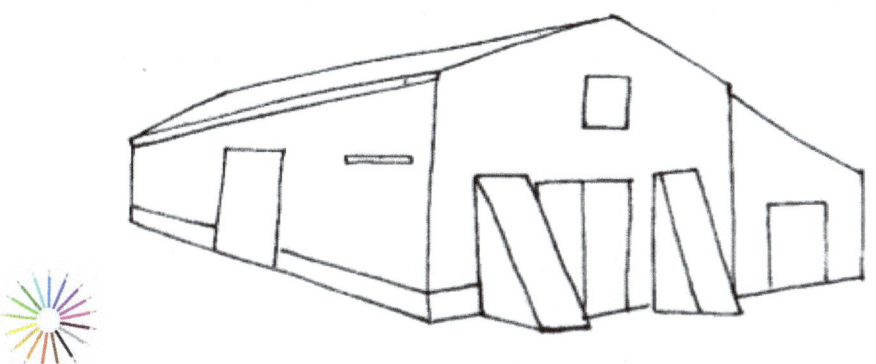

Image 3.3 - Sketch of Old Salt Shed

- Salinas & Windmills - major historic significance to the economy of the Turks and Caicos Islands. The Salt Industry was started by Bermudian Settlers in the 1660s and lasted nearly 300 years. During the dry seasons of the year salt was gathered out of the salinas. The salt was shoveled into bags, stored, and then shipped to customers around the world. Work on the Salinas was originally done by slaves but eventually created many jobs and great income for the Turks and Caicos Islanders.

Image 3.4 - Salinas & Windmills

- St. John's Anglican Church - built in the 1800s by Bermudian Settlers as a place of worship. It is an oceanfront church and graveyard.

Image 3.5 - Sketch of St. John's Anglican Church

ACTIVITY - CHAPTER THREE REVIEW - DIGITAL ART PIECE & LETTER WRITING

A. Compile a photo collage on the island of Salt Cay. Use eight (8) different photos in your collage.

B. Write a letter to your friend telling him/her about the Island.

In order to gather more information, you may visit:

- Turks and Caicos Islands Tourist Board website at https://turksandcaicostourism.com/salt-cay/.
- Visit Turks and Caicos Islands at https://www.visittci.com/salt-cay.
- Turks and Caicos Preservation Foundation at http://www.saltcaypreservation.org/salt-cay-today/

Have you updated your Vocabulary Bank?

CHAPTER FOUR
WELCOME TO SOUTH CAICOS

VOCABULARY BANK REMINDER - As you read through this overview of South Caicos, remember to add any new words and phrases to the vocabulary bank at the back of this book.

Island Overview - The island of South Caicos is:
- known as the 'Fishing Capital' of the Turks and Caicos Islands
- commonly called the "Big South" or "East Harbour"
- located to the immediate west of the Turks Island Passage
- in very close proximity to the uninhabited island of East Caicos
- evidence of the historical Salt Industry of the Turks and Caicos Islands
- 8.5 Square Miles

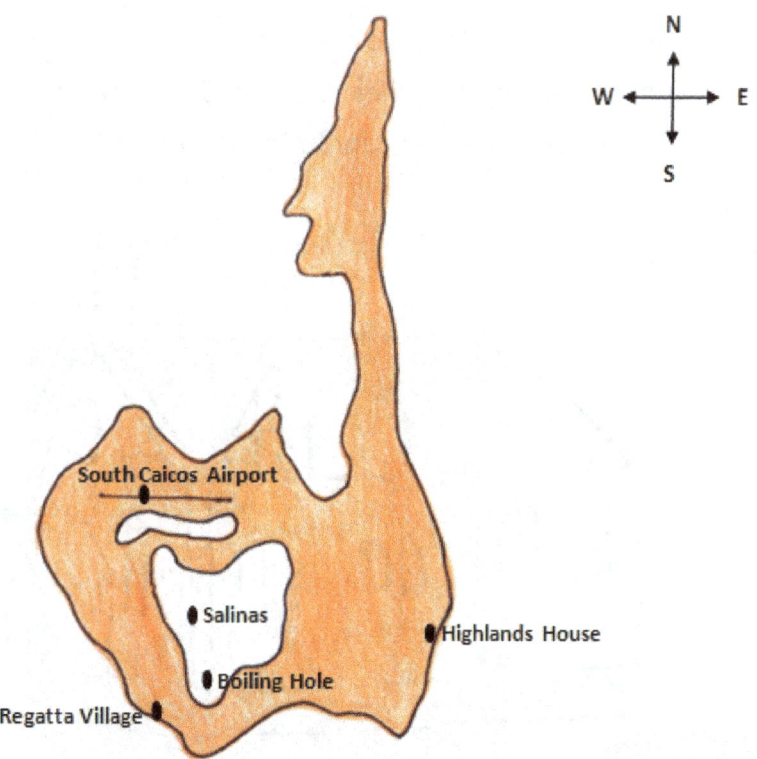

Image 4.1 - Labeled Sketch of South Caicos - South Caicos Airport, Regatta Village, Boiling Hole, Salinas, Highlands House

National Colour - The National Colour chosen for the island of South Caicos is ORANGE. This colour was chosen to represent the orange spiny lobster and other seafood of the Fishing Industry of the "Big South".

Island Festival
- South Caicos Regatta remains the country's oldest Festival. This event commenced in 1966 and has continued throughout the years. It can easily span a 3 - 4-day period with pageants, cultural shows, and concerts being held on separate days.
- Fishermen's Day

Historical Sites - The island of South Caicos is home to the historical sites below. There are also many others to explore. Bring each one to life as you colour.

- St. George's Anglican Church - built at the beginning of the Salt Industry era in the Turks and Caicos Islands. It was most likely built by Bermudian slaves as a place of worship for their owners. It is said to still contain some of the original mahogany furniture installed in the 1800s.

Image 4.2 - Sketch of St. George's Anglican Church

- The Boiling Hole - a gift from nature used to provide saltwater input into the salinas during the Salt Industry. It is a subterranean cave system (cave system that is under the earth) that is connected to the vast ocean around the Turks and Caicos Islands.

Image 4.3 - Sketch of The Boiling Hole

- Old Salt Warehouse - an historic landmark used to store salt that was gathered from the salinas during the 300-year Salt Industry era. This era existed from the 1660s to 1970.

Image 4.4 - Sketch of Old Salt Warehouse

ACTIVITY - CHAPTER FOUR REVIEW - VIDEO REVIEW, POETRY

A. Review the video link below to learn more about South Caicos. This video was published by the Turks and Caicos Islands Tourist Board.

https://www.youtube.com/watch?v=VY080ckMPNs

What new information did you learn?

B. Use your knowledge of South Caicos to write a poem on the island. Your poem should have a minimum of three (3) stanzas.

Share your poem on your social media platform. Title It - "My Poem on "The Big South", South Caicos".

Have you updated your Vocabulary Bank?

CHAPTER FIVE
WELCOME TO MIDDLE CAICOS

VOCABULARY BANK REMINDER - As you read through this overview of Middle Caicos, remember to add any new words and phrases to the vocabulary bank at the back of this book.

Island Overview - The island of Middle Caicos is:
- the largest (square miles) inhabited island in the Turks and Caicos Islands
- located to the west of the Turks Island Passage
- in very close proximity to the uninhabited island of East Caicos
- connected to the island of North Caicos by a Causeway
- evidence of the historical Cotton Industry and Sisal Industry of the Turks and Caicos Islands
- 48 Square Miles

Image 5.1 - Labeled Sketch Of Middle Caicos - Crossing Place Trail, Conch Bar Caves, Indian Cave, Mudjin Harbour, Haulover Estate Plantation, Bambarra, Lorimers, Conch Bar.

National Colour - The National Colour chosen for the island of Middle Caicos is TAN. This colour was chosen to represent the raw 'thatch' that was once used to cover the housetops. This 'thatch' is still used to make straw hats, baskets, and brooms and other craftwork.

Island Festivals - Historically MC Expo has been the Island's festival. The Island is also home to the popular Crab Festival. Middle Caicos is known for the hundreds of crabs that move around the island during the Crab Season.

Historical Facts - The island of Middle Caicos is home to the historical sites below. There are also many others to explore. Bring each one to life as you colour.

- Haulover Estate Plantation - an historical Cotton Plantation and Sisal Plantation located near the settlement of Lomiers. The Plantations were established in 1791 by John Lorimer, a British Military Doctor. In 1807, when Lorimer died, the Plantations became the properties of Wade Stubbs. It is a protected historical site. It is illegal to steal, vandalize or damage any artifact or structure at Haulover Estate Plantation.

Image 5.2 - Sketch of Haulover Estate Plantation

- Conch Bar Caves - a Turks and Caicos Islands Cave System named after the settlement of Conch Bar in which the caves are found. The caves were the site of guano mining in the 1880s. Guano, bat manure, was used as fertilizer. It was mined from the caves and exported to other countries. Hundreds of bats still live in the Conch Bar Caves.

Image 5.3 - Sketch of Conch Bar Caves

- Crossing Place Trail - an historical path that once connected Middle Caicos to North Caicos and by extension the entire Caicos Islands. Users walked this path by foot as there were no motorized vehicles at that time. However, over the years the path was no longer used as bicycles, cars, trucks, and other forms of transportation became popular.

Image 5.4 - Sketch of Crossing Place Trail

ACTIVITY - CHAPTER FIVE REVIEW - STORY WRITING

A. Write a short (3 paragraph) exciting story titled Crab Catching after you review the video found at the link below:

https://www.youtube.com/watch?v=rB1Rg5zKFss

B. Would you want to participate in crab catching?

Have you updated your Vocabulary Bank?

CHAPTER SIX
WELCOME TO NORTH CAICOS

VOCABULARY BANK REMINDER - As you read through this overview of the North Caicos, remember to add any new words and phrases to the vocabulary bank at the back of this book.

Island Overview - The island of North Caicos is:
- known as the 'Garden Island' of the Turks and Caicos Islands
- located to the west of the Turks Island Passage
- connected to the island of Middle Caicos by a Causeway
- evidence of the historical Cotton Industry of the Turks and Caicos Islands
- 41 Square Miles

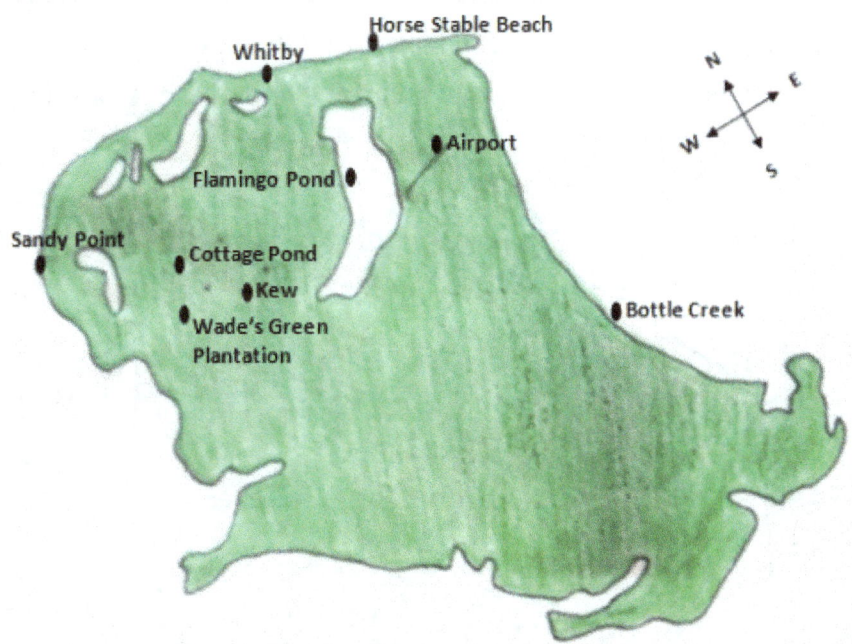

Image 6.1 - Labeled Sketch of North Caicos - Horse Stable Beach, Kew, Whitby, Bottle Creek, Sandy Point, Cottage Pond, Wade's Green Plantation, Flamingo Pond

National Colour - The National Colour chosen for the island of North Caicos is GREEN. This colour was chosen to represent the green fruitfulness of the most fertile land in the Turks and Caicos Islands.

Island Festivals - Historically Festerama has been the Island's festival. The Island is also home to the popular Rake and Scrape Festival. Both events feature live music, island food, and lots of dancing crowds; a great place to meet up with family and friends.

Historical Sites - The island of North Caicos is home to the Wade's Green Plantation Historical Site (see below). Two other places of interest are given below. Bring each one to life as you colour.

- Wade's Green Plantation - an historical Cotton Plantation located in the settlement of Kew. It was established in 1789 by a Loyalist named Wade Stubbs. Buildings at Wade's Green Plantation include the Great House, the kitchen, the overseer's house, slave quarters and storage buildings.

Image 6.2 - Sketch of Wade's Green Plantation

- Cottage Pond - a naturally formed submerged sinkhole located on the Sandy Point Road. This site is the perfect opportunity to see a tropical blue hole opening up to a much larger cave.

Image 6.3 - Sketch of Cottage Pond

- Flamingo Pond - a wetland found off King's Road between Whitby and Horsestable Beach. West Indian Flamingos also known as American Flamingos or Caribbean Flamingos are sometimes seen by the thousands at this protected site. Under the laws of the Turks and Caicos Islands anyone caught harming flamingos, or their eggs will be penalized.

Image 6.4 - Sketch of Flamingo Pond

ACTIVITY - CHAPTER SIX REVIEW - QUESTION & ANSWER EXPLORATORY RESEARCH

A. Visit the website links below and read more about Wade's Green Plantation, Cottage Pond and Flamingo Pond. Then answer the questions that follow.

https://www.visittci.com/wades-green-plantation

https://www.visittci.com/cottage-pond

https://www.visittci.com/flamingo-pond-overlook

1. What is the name of the group that manages Wade's Green Plantation?

2. How many slaves did Wade Stubbs own at the time of his death?

3. What are two (2) other Plantations owned by Wade Stubbs?

4. Why did the Plantation era come to an end?

5. How deep is Cottage Pond?

6. Other than Flamingos, name two (2) other types of birds found in Flamingo Pond.

*** *Confirm that your answers are correct in the Answer Key section at the back.*

Have you updated your Vocabulary Bank?

CHAPTER SEVEN
WELCOME TO PROVIDENCIALES

VOCABULARY BANK REMINDER - As you read through this overview of Providenciales, remember to add any new words and phrases to the vocabulary bank at the back of this book.

Island Overview - The island of Providenciales is:
- known as the 'Tourism Capital' of the Turks and Caicos Islands
- commonly called "Provo"
- the most westerly inhabited island in the archipelago
- in very close proximity to the uninhabited island of West Caicos
- evidence of the historical Cotton Industry of the Turks and Caicos Islands
- 37.5 Square Miles

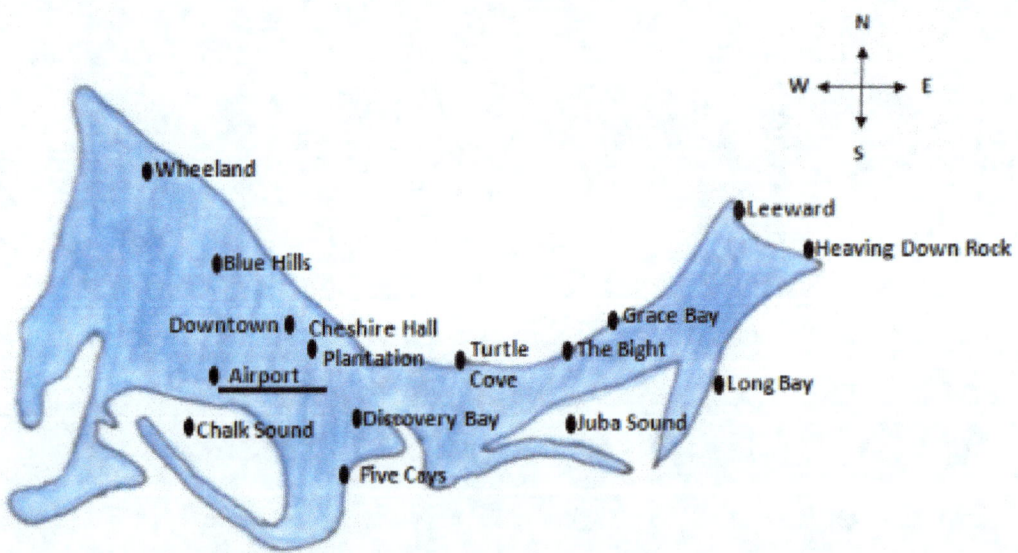

Image 7.1 - Labeled Sketch Of Providenciales - Providenciales International Airport, Five Cays, Blue Hills, The Bight, Discovery Bay, Grace Bay, Leeward, Long Bay, Heaving Down Rock, Cheshire Hall Plantation

National Colour - The National Colour chosen for the island of Providenciales is TURQUOISE. This colour was chosen to represent pristine and beautiful waters surrounding the island; these waters are a major tourist attraction for swimming, snorkeling and other water-based activities.

Island Festivals -
- Providenciales is known for the historical Provo Day activities which have been dormant for many years. The annual activities included Float Parade, Adult Pageant, Children's Pageant, and Live Entertainment.
- Around 2005 The Turks and Caicos Islands Music and Cultural Festival emerged and featured a slate of international and local artists, along with some aspects of the Provo Day activities.
- In 2010 Maskanoo, held on December 26th, Boxing Day, joined Providenciales Festivals.

Historical Sites - The island of Providenciales is home to the historical sites below. There are also many other modern attractions to visit. Bring each one to life as you colour.

- Cheshire Hall Plantation - an historical Cotton Plantation located near DownTown. It was established in the 1700s by a Loyalist named Thomas Stubbs (brother to Wade Stubbs of Wade's Green Plantation, Kew, North Caicos). Thomas Stubbs eventually sold Cheshire Hall Plantation to his brother Wade in 1810.

Image 7.2 - Sketch of Cheshire Hall Plantation

- National Museum and Heritage Site - this site is located in the Grace Bay area and hosts a small collection of outdoor historical exhibits. It is the counterpart to the Turks and Caicos National Museum on Grand Turk.

Image 7.3 - Sketch of National Museum and Heritage Site

ACTIVITY - CHAPTER SEVEN REVIEW - CREATIVE WRITING (JINGLE) & EXPLORATORY RESEARCH

A. Visit the website link below and read about a "Family and Kids 7 Day Itinerary" for persons who vacation in Providenciales.

https://www.visittci.com/providenciales/itineraries/one-week-first-time-visitors-itinerary

B. Compose a catchy 60 second jingle that can be used to advertise this itinerary to families and kids.

C. Record your jingle and post on your social media pages.
Have you updated your Vocabulary Bank?

CHAPTER EIGHT
WELCOME TO OUR TOURISM CAYS -
PARROT CAY, PINE CAY, AMBERGRIS CAY

VOCABULARY BANK REMINDER - As you read through this overview of the Tourism Cays, remember to add any new words and phrases to the vocabulary bank at the back of this book.

Island Overview - The island of Parrot Cay is:
- located to the immediate west of North Caicos
- a private island resort (COMO Parrot Cay Resort, along with exclusive rental villas and residences) accessible by privately scheduled boats
- ascribed Green as its National Colour (along with the neighbouring North Caicos)
- originally named 'Pirate Cay' due to pirates hiding out in the location the 1600s - 1700s

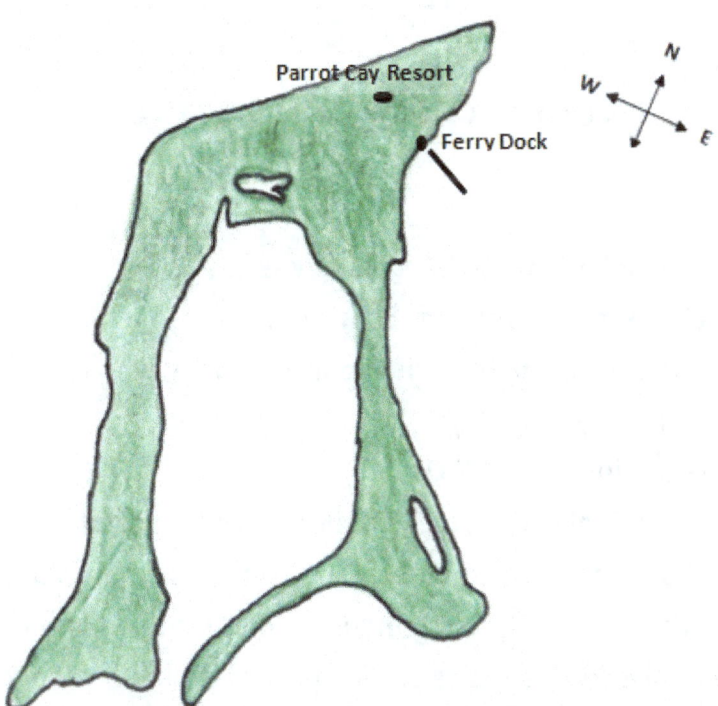

Image 8.1 - Coloured Sketch of Parrot Cay

Island Overview - The island of Pine Cay is:
- privately owned and has low-density development
- home to the Meridian Club Resort, private residences, and villas
- named after the endemic Caicos Pine
- home to a private airstrip for private planes and chartered flights; also accessible by privately scheduled boats
- 15-minute boat ride from Providenciales
- ascribed Turquoise as its National Colour (along with the neighbouring Providenciales)

Image 8.2 - Coloured Sketch of Pine Cay

Island Overview - The island of Ambergris Cay is:
- approximately 14 miles north of South Caicos
- named after the whale ambergris (vomited up my whales) that washed up on the shore of the cay
- privately owned since the 1800s
- operated by the Turks and Caicos Collection as a private residential luxury island since 2018; accessible by privately scheduled aircrafts
- evidence of the historic whaling industry and sisal industry
- home to several endangered species, some of which are only found in the Turks and Caicos Islands. These include the Rock Iguana and the Turks Head Cactus

- ascribed Orange as its National Colour (along with the neighbouring South Caicos)

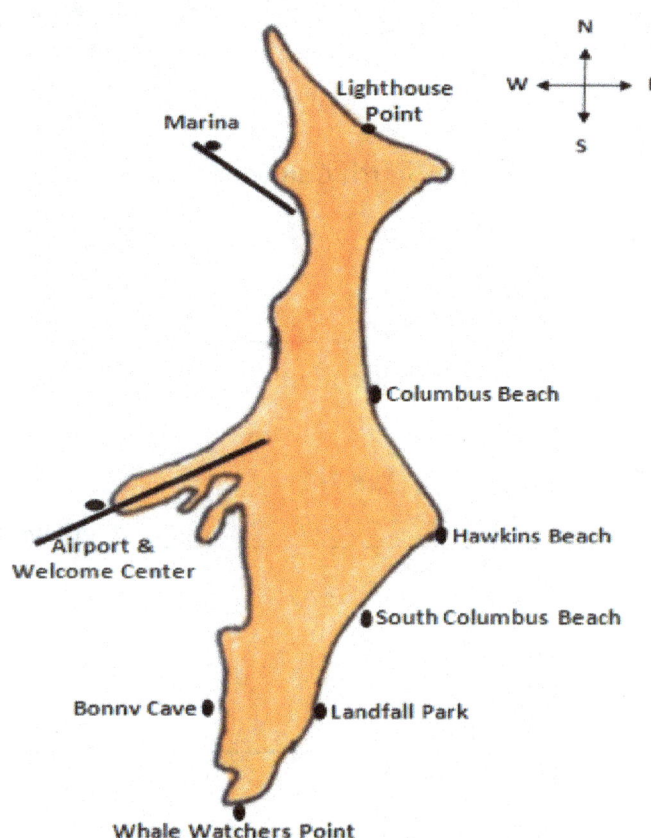

Image 8.3 - Coloured Sketch of Ambergris Cay

ACTIVITY - CHAPTER EIGHT REVIEW - FILL-IN-THE-BLANK

A. Complete the statements below by filling in the blanks.

1. _____ is located immediately west of North Caicos.

2. The national colour ascribed to _____ is turquoise.

3. The Rock Iguana and Turks Head Cactus are found on _____.

4. _____ is home to Meridian Club and has a private airstrip.

5. Approximately 14 miles of South Caicos is _____.

6. Parrot Cay was originally named _____ and has been ascribed the national colour _____.

7. Ambergris Cay was named after the _____ that washed up on the shoreline.

8. Pine Cay is named after the _____.

*** Confirm that your answers are correct in the Answer Key section at the back.

Have you updated your Vocabulary Bank?

MY VOCABULARY BANK (NEW WORDS & PHRASES)

ANSWER KEY

CHAPTER ONE

A. Fill in the Blanks
1. Southeast
2. United States Dollar (US Dollar, American Dollar)
3. Atlantic Ocean
4. Peas & Hominy
5. *Any of the following is correct:* Providenciales International Airport, JAGS International Airport, South Caicos International Airport, Grand Turk Cruise Center
6. *Any of the following is correct:* Pine Cay, Parrot Cay or Ambergris Cay

CHAPTER SIX

A. Exploratory Research Responses
1. Turks and Caicos National Trust
2. 384 slaves
3. Haulover Plantation on Middle Caicos, and Cheshire Hall on Providenciales
4. Soil degradation, plant diseases and insects, and changes in the world markets
5. 250 feet deep
6. *Any two (2) of the following are correct:* spoonbills, ducks, stilts, herons, and egrets

CHAPTER EIGHT

B. Fill in the Blanks
1. Parrot Cay
2. Pine Cay
3. Ambergris Cay
4. Pine Cay
5. Ambergris Cay
6. Pirate Cay, Green
7. Whale Ambergris (vomited up by whales)
8. Caicos Pine

OUR TEAM

Author/Assistant Illustrator: Desiree Adams Robinson

Desiree was born on the island of Grand Turk and presently resides on the island of Providenciales. After completing Primary and Secondary School in the TCI she pursued a Certificate in Food & Beverage Management and a Diploma in Hotel Management at the University of Technology, Jamaica. She completed her Bachelor Degree in Hospitality Management at Johnson and Wales University and her Masters in Business Administration (Management) at the University of Tampa. Professionally, she has worked in Hospitality, Tourism, and Education. Since 2018 she has been an entrepreneur of Desiree Adams Training (DAT). She loves God sincerely and wishes for family, friends, and all others to succeed in their life's calling.

Editor: Jason Henry

Jason Henry is a Jamaican native who has lived and worked in the Turks and Caicos since 2010. He has a Bachelor of Arts Degree in Literatures in English, Postgraduate Diploma in Language Education and a Masters Degree in Language Education – all from The University of the West Indies (Mona). An educator of adolescents and adults for over 22 years, Jason has dedicated his professional life in service in education as a vehicle for transformational and positive social change.

Chief Illustrator: Kendra Malcolm

Kendra O. Malcolm is a native of the Turks and Caicos Islands. During her early school years at the Mary Robinson Primary School in Salt Cay, she developed an eye for Art and began entering Art Competitions in both Primary and High School. After High School, Kendra became engaged in representing the TCI in Art Exhibits and Cultural Shows. She specializes in landscape art, portraits, designs for banners, signs, building art-work, wood burning, costume designs and recently became known for graphic designing. Mediums she enjoys using include oil, water and spray paint, cardboard, canvas, paper collage, clay, recycled bottles and many more. She is inspired by everyday life (nature) and the lost culture of the TCI.

www.ingramcontent.com/pod-product-compliance
Lightning Source LLC
Chambersburg PA
CBHW081356080526
44588CB00016B/2520